Modern American English

Robert J. Dixson
As Revised by Eugene J. Hall

New Edition

REGENTS/PRENTICE HALL
Englewood Cliffs, New Jersey 07632

Library of Congress Cataloging-in-Publication Data

Dixson, Robert James.
Modern American English / Robert J. Dixson. — New ed.
ISBN 0-13-593914-3 (v. 1)
    1. English language—Textbooks for foreign speakers. 2. English
language—Grammar—1950– 3. English language—United States.
I. Title.
PE1128.D515 1992
428.2'4—dc20   92–7104
                                              CIP

Publisher: Tina B. Carver
Manager of Product Development: Mary Vaughn
Development Editor: Louisa B. Hellegers
Senior Production Editor: Tunde A. Dewey
Interior design and page layout: Function Through Form
Design supervision: Janet Schmid and Chris Wolf
Pre-press buyer: Ray Keating
Manufacturing buyer: Lori Bulwin

Cover design: Bruce Kenselaar
Cover photograph: © John Kelly/The Image Bank

Illustrations by Anna Veltfort

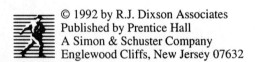

© 1992 by R.J. Dixson Associates
Published by Prentice Hall
A Simon & Schuster Company
Englewood Cliffs, New Jersey 07632

Printed in the United States of America

10 9 8 7 6 5 4 3

ISBN 0-13-593914-3

Prentice-Hall International (UK) Limited, *London*
Prentice-Hall of Australia Pty. Limited, *Sydney*
Prentice-Hall Canada Inc., *Toronto*
Prentice-Hall Hispanoamericana, S.A., *Mexico*
Prentice-Hall of India Private Limited, *New Delhi*
Prentice-Hall of Japan, Inc., *Tokyo*
Simon & Schuster Asia Pte. Ltd., *Singapore*
Editora Prentice-Hall do Brasil, Ltda., *Rio de Janeiro*

Contents

Preface

Modern American English 1 is the first of a series of six texts, with correlated workbooks and cassettes, designed as a complete course of study in English as a second language. This book provides elementary vocabulary and lays the foundations for a comprehension of the first principles of English grammar. Books 2, 3, 4, 5, the workbooks, and the cassettes build upon this foundation by expanding the study of vocabulary and completing the survey of English grammatical structure. Book 6, although primarily a reader, provides a general review and additional practice on all the material in books 1 through 5.

The six books of the series have been planned for use in the junior high school, high school, or adult course of study. The pace of the books is measured but intensive, as is proper for students studying English on this level. Extensive oral practice is provided for everything presented. Students are prepared to move, without difficulty or confusion, from one step to the next, from one lesson to the following lesson. Vocabulary and grammar are controlled at all times, particularly at the beginning and intermediate levels in books 1 through 4. Consequently, there is no danger of teaching more vocabulary or structure than a student can readily absorb.

Expressed in a different way, the purpose of this book, as well as of the remaining books of the series, is to teach students how to use and understand spoken English. The approach emphasizes at all times the ability of the students to use what they have studied. All materials and all activities in the series contribute directly to this end.

Modern American English 1 is simple to use and easy to follow. It is a basic book, consisting of fifteen lessons. Every fifth lesson is a review that provides additional practice on the material covered in the previous four lessons. Each of the remaining lessons is divided into four sections: *Reading and Oral Practice; Structure and Pattern Practice; Pronunciation and Intonation Practice;* and *General Practice.* (The pronunciation material is omitted in Lesson One.) Each of these sections is intended to give a particular kind of practice that will strengthen the students' learning experience and lead to their ability to communicate in the new language.

1. Reading and Oral Practice. This section introduces the material to be studied in the lesson. It usually consists of a series of questions and answers cued to pictures. As more structures and vocabulary are presented, this introductory material is usually connected into a brief narrative. Many of the lessons present both structural material—verb tenses, possessive forms, and so on—and cultural material—telling time, days of the week, months of the year, and so on. In addition, short dialogues beginning with Lesson Eight introduce the students to such conversational forms as greetings and leave-takings. Notes on idiomatic and cultural material are introduced at the end of the section in which expressions of this kind are first used.

The first part of each section is intended primarily for listening and repeating practice. That is, the students should listen while the teacher reads the sentences; then the students should repeat them in chorus after the teacher; third, individual students should be asked to repeat both questions and answers; and finally, individual students should read the sentences, both questions and answers.

In the next section, the students answer questions based on the previous material that are cued to the same or similar pictures. The teacher should first go over this section as a listening practice, giving both questions and answers; choral and individual repetition should follow; then the teacher should ask the questions while individual students give the answers. As a final step, one student asks the questions and another student gives the answers. This kind of student-student practice is highly recommended for all the exercises throughout the book.

In general, the structural and the cultural material is presented separately but in the same manner—that is, with a listen and repeat practice first and a question and answer practice second.

Similar procedures should be followed for the dialogues—listening, choral and individual repetition, teacher-student practice, and student-student practice.

2. **Structure and Pattern Practice.** This section is devoted to the study of grammatical structures and patterns in English. First, explanatory notes on the structure or structures are presented in the lesson. Each note is followed by one or more exercises to give the students practice on the pattern discussed in the preceding note. The exercises are intended to help the students achieve command of the formal features of English.

It is suggested that the teacher first go through each exercise orally, with students repeating each cue and its answer in chorus. In the next step, the teacher should present the cue and then ask the class to give the answer in chorus. After that, the teacher should give the cue, with individual students giving the answer. Wrong answers should be corrected immediately with the right ones, which the students should then repeat in chorus.

When sufficient oral work has been done, the teacher can assign the exercises as written homework. Homework should be corrected carefully and returned to the students so that they can note their errors and observe their progress. The exercises in this section are designed for habit formation on specific patterns, whereas the conversation practice in the final section of the lesson is designed to give the students greater flexibility in the *use* of the patterns.

3. **Pronunciation and Intonation Practice.** This section gives practice on different aspects of pronunciation. Drills are given on the pronunciation of individual vowels and consonants. Special practice is also included on points that may be difficult for some students, such as the different pronunciations of the *s* and *d* endings. Intonation practice is provided through special exercises marked with intonation patterns.

The material in this section should be presented by means of choral and individual repetition. The teacher's pronunciation and intonation will serve as a model for the students. The sentences for intonation practice should be said at a natural conversational speed so that the students will become accustomed to the sound of English as it is actually spoken. The cassettes give valuable additional practice for this section.

4. **General Practice.** This section gives oral practice in the actual use of English for conversational purposes. Several of the exercises are question and answer practices based on the material presented previously in the lesson. The questions are cued to visual information for which verbal equivalents are to be given. Procedures should consist first of teacher-student practice, in which the teacher asks the questions and indi-

vidual students respond. Second should be student-student practice, in which one student acts as teacher and another makes the appropriate responses.

Beginning with Lesson Four, the given questions should be used for controlled conversation practice. These are questions that the students can answer from their own experience and knowledge within the structural and cultural framework of the patterns and vocabulary that have been studied. These exercises are only suggestions. Each teacher should work out the particular exercise, with appropriate questions and commands, before giving it to the students, so that it will conform to the reality of the particular classroom and group of students.

SUPPLEMENTARY MATERIAL. A Teacher's Edition is available for each level of this series. For each book, a companion workbook is available in which each lesson is closely coordinated with the corresponding material in its matching book. The workbooks provide additional material to help build all four language skills: listening, speaking, reading, and writing. For even more oral practice, cassettes may be obtained that cover the material in each of the book lessons.

1

O N E

Reading and Oral Practice

A. Listen and repeat.

Michael is a student.
He is a student.

Susan is a student.
She is a student.

Mrs. Jones is a teacher.
She is a teacher.

Sam Stern is a doctor.
He is a doctor.

Bill is a salesclerk.
He is a salesclerk.

Kay Williams is a lawyer.
She is a lawyer.

Kevin is a cook.
He is a cook.

Amy is a cashier.
She is a cashier.

Marta is a typist.
She is a typist.

Ed is a driver.
He is a driver.

Mrs. is a title that is used for a married woman.

B. Answer the questions.

Is Michael a teacher or a student?
He is a student.

1. Is Susan a student or a lawyer?

2. Is Mrs. Jones a teacher or a student?

3. Is Sam Stern a lawyer or a doctor?

4. Is Bill a cashier or a salesclerk?

5. Is Kay Williams a lawyer or a doctor?

6. Is Kevin a cook or a driver?

7. Is Amy a lawyer or a cashier?

8. Is Marta a typist or a salesclerk?

9. Is Ed a cook or a driver?

C. Listen and repeat.

Is Michael a teacher?
No, he is not a teacher.
Is he a college student?
Yes, he is a college student.

Is Susan a salesclerk?
No, she is not a salesclerk.
Is she a college student?
Yes, she is a college student.

Is Mrs. Jones a typist?
No, she is not a typist.
Is she a teacher?
Yes, she is a teacher.

Is Sam Stern a lawyer?
No, he is not a lawyer.
Is he a doctor?
Yes, he is a doctor.

Is Bill a driver?
No, he is not a driver.
Is he a salesclerk?
Yes, he is a salesclerk.

Is Amy a cook?
No, she is not a cook.
Is she a cashier?
Yes, she is a cashier.

College in American English refers to a university, not a high school.

Structure and Pattern Practice

> *Is* is a form of the verb *to be*. In statements it is used after a singular noun (*Michael, Susan*) or after *he* or *she*.
>
> > Michael is a college student.
> > He is a college student.
> >
> > Mrs. Jones is a teacher.
> > She is a teacher.
>
> The negative is formed by placing *not* after *is*.
>
> > Sam Stern is not a lawyer.
> > She is not a teacher.

A. Change the name in each sentence to *he* or *she*.

EXAMPLE

Michael is a college student.   *He is a college student.*

1. Mrs. Jones is a teacher.
2. Amy is a cashier.
3. Kevin is a cook.
4. Ed is a driver.
5. Kay Williams is a lawyer.
6. Sam Stern is a doctor.

B. Change to the negative.

EXAMPLE

Susan is a teacher.   *Susan is not a teacher.*

1. Kay Williams is a typist.
2. Michael is a salesclerk.
3. Amy is a lawyer.
4. Bill is a cashier.
5. Mrs. Jones is a college student.
6. Ed is a cook.

> Questions that ask for *Yes* or *No* as the answer are
> formed by placing *is* at the beginning of the
> sentence, before the subject.
>
> Michael is a college student.
> Is Michael a college student?
> Is he a college student?
>
> Kay Williams is a lawyer.
> Is Kay Williams a lawyer?
> Is she a lawyer?

C. Change to questions.

EXAMPLE

Michael is a college student.   *Is Michael a college student?*

1. He is a salesclerk.
2. Marta is a typist.
3. Sam Stern is a doctor.
4. She is a lawyer.
5. Ed is a driver.
6. She is a cashier.

D. Change to statements.

EXAMPLE

Is Susan a college student?   *Susan is a college student.*

1. Is Mrs. Jones a teacher?
2. Is Kevin a cook?
3. Is Marta a typist?
4. Is Kay Williams a lawyer?
5. Is Ed a driver?
6. Is Sam Stern a doctor?

General Practice

Answer the questions. Use *he* or *she*.

Is Mrs. Jones a teacher or a lawyer?
She is a teacher.   She is not a lawyer.

1. Is Susan a college student or a teacher?

2. Is Ed a driver or a cook?

3. Is Bill a salesclerk or a cook?

4. Is Kay Williams a lawyer or a salesclerk?

5. Is Marta a typist or a cashier?

6. Is Sam Stern a doctor or a lawyer?

T W O

Reading and Oral Practice

A. Listen and repeat.

I am a student.

You are a student.

We are students.

I am a teacher.

You are students.

Miss Lopez is a nurse.
She is a nurse.

Mrs. Nakama is also a nurse.

Miss Lopez and Mrs. Nakama are nurses.
They are nurses.

Mr. Lee is a lawyer.
He is a lawyer.

Ms. Williams is a lawyer.
She is a lawyer.

Mr. Lee and Ms. Williams are lawyers.
They are lawyers.

Mr., *Mrs.*, *Miss*, and *Ms.* are titles of address. *Mr.* is used for a man, *Mrs.* for a married woman, *Miss* for an unmarried woman, and *Ms.* for either a married or unmarried woman. *Dr.* is another title of address, used for a medical doctor or dentist.

B. Answer the questions.

Are you a student or a teacher?
I am a student.

1. Are you students or teachers? (We)

2. Is Michael a student or a lawyer?

3. Is Miss Lopez a salesclerk or a nurse?

4. Am I a doctor or a typist? (You)

5. Are we typists or cooks? (You)

6. Are Miss Lopez and Mrs. Nakama teachers or nurses?

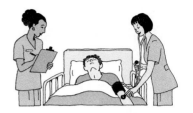

7. Is Amy a cashier or a nurse?

8. Are Susan and Michael students or teachers?

9. Is Ms. Williams a lawyer or a nurse?

10. Is Mr. Lee a lawyer or a teacher?

11. Are Ms. Williams and Mr. Lee doctors or lawyers?

Answers to yes-no questions are often shortened to *yes* plus a pronoun subject and the appropriate form of *to be*.

Is Mrs. Jones a teacher? Yes, she is.
Are you typists? Yes, we are.

C. Answer the questions.

EXAMPLE

Are you a student? (I)
Yes, I am.

---

1. Is Susan a college student?

---

2. Are you students? (we)

---

3. Is Kevin a cook?

---

4. Are Susan and Michael college students?

---

5. Are Miss Lopez and Mrs. Nakama nurses?

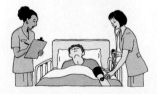

D. Listen and repeat.

What is this?
It is a book.
What color is it?
It is white.

What is this?
It is a pencil.
What color is it?
It is yellow.

What is this?
It is a pen.
What color is it?
It is blue.

What is this?
It is a chair.
What color is it?
It is brown.

What is this?
It is a bus.
What color is it?
It is green.

What are these?
They are books.
What color are they?
They are red.

What are these?
They are pencils.
What color are they?
They are yellow.

What are these?
They are pens.
What color are they?
They are black.

What are these?
They are chairs.
What color are they?
They are brown.

What are these?
They are buses.
What color are they?
They are green.

What is this? asks for one object to be identified.
What are these? asks for two or more objects to be
identified.

What is this?	What are these?
It is a chair.	They are chairs.

What color is it? asks for one object to be
described. *What color are they?* asks for two or
more objects to be described. Notice that the
color adjective is the same in both the singular
and the plural.

What color is it?	What color are they?
It is yellow.	They are yellow.

E. Answer the questions.

What is this?   *It is a book.*
What color is it?   *It is red.*

1. What are these?
   What color are they?

2. What is this?
   What color is it?

3. What are these?
   What color are they?

4. What is this?
   What color is it?

5. What are these?
   What color are they?

Structure and Pattern Practice

> *Am* and *are* are the other forms of the present
> tense of the verb *to be*. All the forms are:
>
> | *Singular* | *Plural* |
> |---|---|
> | I am | we are |
> | you are | you are |
> | he, she, it is | they are |

A. Answer the questions.

EXAMPLE

Is Mr. Lee a doctor or a lawyer?
He is a lawyer.

1. Is Michael a student or a teacher?

2. Are you a student or a teacher? (I)

3. Am I a teacher or a student? (You)

18

4. Is Bill a salesclerk or a typist?

5. Are Miss Lopez and Mrs. Nakama nurses or doctors?

6. Are you students or teachers? (we)

7. Are these pencils or pens?

8. Are we students or teachers? (you)

9. Is Ms. Williams a lawyer or a doctor?

10. Is this a pencil or a pen?

Most nouns in English form the plural by adding *s* to the singular.

Singular	*Plural*
student	students
book	books

Note that the plural of *bus* is *buses*. In both *buses* and *nurses* the plural ending is pronounced as a separate syllable.

Note that *a* is used only with a singular noun.

He is a lawyer.   They are lawyers.

B. Change to the plural.

EXAMPLE

He is a doctor.   *They are doctors.*

1. I am a typist.
2. I am a student.
3. You are a teacher.
4. It is a chair.
5. She is a nurse.
6. It is a pen.
7. He is a driver.
8. She is a lawyer.

C. Change to the singular.

EXAMPLE

They are doctors. (she)   *She is a doctor.*

1. They are books. (it)
2. They are cooks. (he)
3. They are buses. (it)
4. We are nurses. (I)
5. You are teachers. (you)
6. They are typists. (he)
7. They are teachers. (she)
8. We are students. (I)

Pronunciation and Intonation Practice

A. The indefinite article *a* is pronounced like the *u* in *bus*. Repeat several times.

a book   *a* teacher
a doctor   *a* pen
a chair   *a* lawyer

B. Final *s* is pronounced *s* in some words, but in other words it is pronounced *z*. Repeat several times.

s	*z*
book, books	doctor, doctors
student, students	teacher, teachers
typist, typists	pen, pens

C. Listen and repeat.

EXAMPLE

(TEACHER)   Mr. Lee is a lawyer.

(STUDENTS)   Mr. Lee is a lawyer.

(TEACHER)   Mr. Lee is a lawyer.

1. They are nurses.
2. We are students.
3. Michael and I are students.
4. Sam Stern is a doctor.
5. Mrs. Nakama is a nurse.

General Practice

Answer the questions.

EXAMPLE

Is this a book?
Yes, it is a book.

Is this a book?
Yes, it is also a book.
They are books.

1. Is Nora a typist?

   Is Marta a typist?

2. Are you a student?

   Is Susan a student?

3. Is Mr. Lee a lawyer?

   Is Ms. Williams a
   lawyer?

4. Is this a bus?

   Is this a bus?

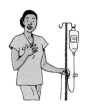

5. Am I a nurse?

      Is Mrs. Nakama a nurse?

6. Is this a pencil?

      Is this a pencil?

7. Is Mrs. Nakama a nurse?

      Is Miss Lopez a nurse?

8. Is Susan a student?

      Is Michael a student?

9. Is this a pen?

      Is this a pen?

10. Is this a chair?

      Is this a chair?

3

Reading and Oral Practice

A. Listen and repeat.

This is a map.

That is a chalkboard.

This is a door.
That is a window.

This is a notebook.

That is a desk.

That is a table.

 These are windows.

 Those are doors.

 These are desks.

 Those are maps.

 These are tables.

 Those are notebooks.

B. Answer the questions.

What is this?
This is a book.

1. What is that?

2. What is this?

3. What is that?

4. What are these?

5. What is this?

6. What are those?

7. What is this?

8. What are these?

9. What is that?

10. What are these?

11. What are those?

C. Answer the questions.

EXAMPLE

Is this a book?
No, it is not a book.   It is a pen.

1. Is this a pencil?

2. Are these maps?

3. Are those windows?

4. Is that a table?

5. Are these doors?

Structure and Pattern Practice

DEMONSTRATIVES. *This* is singular and indicates something close to the speaker. *These* is plural and also indicates something close to the speaker.

That is singular and indicates something farther away from the speaker. *Those* is plural and also indicates something farther away from the speaker.

This, these, that, and *those* are used both as pronouns and adjectives.

A. Change to the plural.

EXAMPLE

This is a book.   *These are books.*

1. That is a chalkboard.
2. That is a pen.
3. This is a door.
4. That is a window.
5. That is a desk.
6. This is a map.
7. That is a bus.
8. This is a bus.
9. This is a pencil.
10. That is a chair.
11. That is a notebook.
12. This is a table.
13. This is a pen.
14. This is a chair.
15. That is a map.

CONTRACTIONS. In everyday conversation we customarily use the following contracted forms of *to be*:

I'm (I am)	we're (we are)
you're (you are)	you're (you are)
he's (he is)	
she's (she is) }	they're (they are)
it's (it is)	

Other common contractions are:

what's (what is)   that's (that is)

B. Change to the contracted forms.

EXAMPLE

He is a student.   *He's a student.*

1. They are windows.
2. She is a doctor.
3. They are nurses.
4. You are a teacher.
5. We are lawyers.
6. That is a chalkboard.
7. You are typists.
8. I am a salesclerk.
9. It is a map.
10. What is this?
11. He is a driver.
12. It is a pen.
13. They are pencils.
14. He is a cook.
15. She is a cashier.

NEGATIVE. Remember that *not* is placed after the form of *to be* in the negative.

I'm not	we're not
you're not	you're not
he's not	
she's not }	they're not
it's not	

C. Change to the negative. Use the contracted forms.

EXAMPLE

He's a teacher.   *He's not a teacher.*

1. They're maps.
2. It's a notebook.
3. We're lawyers.
4. He's a cook.
5. She's a salesclerk.
6. You're a nurse.
7. You're drivers.
8. I'm a typist.

QUESTIONS. In questions, the form of *to be* comes before the subject.

Am I . . . ?	Are we . . . ?
Are you . . . ?	Are you . . . ?
Is he . . . ?	
Is she . . . ? }	Are they . . . ?
Is it . . . ?	

D. Change to questions.

EXAMPLE

He's a doctor.   *Is he a doctor?*

1. It's a table.
2. She's a lawyer.
3. I'm a salesclerk. (you)
4. It's a door.
5. We're students. (you)
6. They're nurses.
7. He's a cashier.
8. They're desks.

Pronunciation and Intonation Practice

A. Listen and repeat.

EXAMPLE

(TEACHER)   He's a doctor.

(STUDENTS)   He's a doctor.

(TEACHER)   He's a doctor.

1. It's a door.
2. She's a nurse.
3. I'm a student.
4. It's a book.
5. They're salesclerks.
6. That's a pencil.
7. He's a driver.
8. Those are chalkboards.
9. She's a lawyer.
10. We're students.
11. That's a window.
12. This is a pen.

B. Repeat several times.

e as in *he*:   she, we, teacher, she's, he's
i as in *is*:   this, it, Bill, Miss
z as in *is*:   he's, she's, pens, doctors, cashiers
s as in *this*:   nurse, books, students, typists

General Practice

Answer the questions. Use the contracted forms.

EXAMPLE

Is she a teacher?
No, she's not a teacher.   She's a nurse.

1. Is this a window?

2. Is she a doctor?

3. Is that a chalkboard?

4. Are these pens?

5. Are you a cashier? (I)

6. Is he a typist?

LESSON

4

FOUR

Reading and Oral Practice

A. Listen and repeat.

1
Where is your book?
My book is on my desk.

2
Where is my book?
Your book is on your desk.

3
Where are your books?
Our books are on the floor.

4
Where are our books?
Your books are on the table.

5
Where is his book?
His book is on the chair.

Where is her book?
Her book is on her desk.

6

Where are their books?
Their books are on the floor.

7

Where is her purse?
Her purse is on her desk.

8

Where are their purses?
Their purses are on their desks.

9

Where is your notebook?
My notebook is on my desk.

10

Where are your notebooks?
Our notebooks are on the table.

11

B. Answer the questions.

Where is his pen?
His pen is on the table.

1. Where is your notebook? (my)

2. Where is her purse?

3. Where are your books? (our)

4. Where are his books?

5. Where are their notebooks?

6. Where is my notebook? (your)

7. Where are her pencils?

8. Where is your pen? (my)

9. Where is my pen? (your)

10. Where are our pens? (your)

11. Where are their purses?

C. Listen and repeat.

1

What's this?
It's a clock.

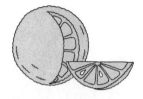

2

What's this?
It's an orange.

3

What's this?
It's a map.

4

What's this?
It's an apple.

5

What's this?
It's a new car.

6

What's this?
It's an old car.

D. Answer the questions.

EXAMPLE

Is this a new book or an old book?
It's an old book.   It's not a new book.

1. Is this an apple or an orange?

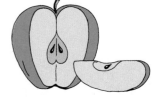

2. Is this a new car or an old car?

3. Is this a pen or an orange?

4. Is this a map or a clock?

5. Is this a new pencil or an old pencil?

6. Is this a map or a bus?

Structure and Pattern Practice

> The possessive adjectives in English are used before nouns. They are:
>
> | Singular | Plural |
> |----------|--------|
> | I – my | we – our |
> | you – your | you – your |
> | he – his | they – their |
> | she – her | |
>
> They are used before both singular and plural nouns.
>
> My book is on my desk.   My books are on my desk.

A. Complete these sentences with the possessive adjective that refers to the subject of the first sentence.

EXAMPLE

Michael is a college student. _____His_____ book is on the chair.

1. Mrs. Jones is a teacher. _____ pen is on the desk.
2. Susan and Michael are college students. _____ books are on the floor.
3. I'm a teacher. _____ pencil is on the desk.
4. You're a student. _____ notebook is on the chair.
5. We're teachers. _____ books are on the table.
6. Sam Stern is a doctor. _____ pen is on the floor.

> A and an are called indefinite articles. They refer only to words in the singular. A is used before words that begin with a consonant sound. An is used before words that begin with a vowel sound.
>
> It's a book.   It's an orange.
>
> The is called the definite article. It can be used before either singular or plural nouns.
>
> The books are on the floor.   The book is on the floor.

Descriptive adjectives like *new* and *old* come before the nouns they describe. Adjectives have no plural form in English.

It's a new car.   They're new cars.
It's an old book.   They're old books.

B. Add *old* to these sentences and make any other changes that are necessary.

EXAMPLE

It's a table.   *It's an old table.*

1. They're chairs.   4. They're clocks.
2. It's a car.   5. It's a notebook.
3. It's a chair.   6. They're books.

Where is a question word that asks for place or location. It is often contracted with *is* to form *where's*.

Where's your book?   It's on my desk.

C. Answer the questions.

EXAMPLE

Where's his book?
His book is on the floor.

1. Where are her pencils?

2. Where's your notebook? (my)

3. Where are their books?

4. Where are our notebooks? (your)

5. Where's my book? (your)

6. Where are your pencils? (our)

7. Where are her books?

8. Where's his notebook?

Pronunciation and Intonation Practice

A. Listen and repeat.

EXAMPLE

(TEACHER)   It's a new book.

1. It's his book.
2. It's an old chair.
3. It's an old car.
4. It's her pen.
5. It's a new map.

B. Repeat several times.

a as in *am*:   apple, and, map, that
o as in *not*:   clock, on
  z as in *is*:   these, those, he's, she's, pens, apples, doctors
s as in *this*:   nurse, student, Sam Stern, clocks, Miss

General Practice

Conversation. Your teacher will ask you these questions or others like them. The questions will ask about things you can see or things you know about from your own experience. Give *real* answers to the questions.

Is that your book or your notebook?
Where's your book?
Is that your notebook or your book?
Where's your notebook?
Is that your pen or your pencil?
Where's your pen?
Is that your pencil or your pen?
Where's your pencil?

REVIEW

Structure and Pattern Practice

A. Change to the negative. Use the contracted forms.

EXAMPLE

He's a cook.   *He's not a cook.*

1. It's an orange.
2. She's a nurse.
3. I'm a doctor.
4. It's a new clock.
5. They're drivers.
6. You're a lawyer.
7. We're cashiers.
8. You're teachers.

B. Change to questions.

EXAMPLE

He's a college student.   *Is he a college student?*

1. It's a new pen.
2. I'm a teacher. (you)
3. She's a salesclerk.
4. That's an old clock.
5. We're students. (you)
6. These are oranges.
7. It's a new table.
8. They're doctors.

C. Change to the plural. Use the contracted forms.

EXAMPLE

He's a lawyer.   *They're lawyers.*

1. It's a new car.
2. I'm a teacher.
3. It's a map.

4. She's a nurse.
5. It's an old bus.

D. Change to the singular. Use the contracted forms.

EXAMPLE

They're lawyers. (he)   *He's a lawyer.*

1. They're doctors. (she)
2. We're nurses.
3. They're typists. (he)

4. You're students.
5. They're teachers. (she)

E. Change to the plural.

EXAMPLE

This is a book.   *These are books.*

1. That's a window.
2. That's an old chair.
3. This is a red pen.

4. This is a blue pencil.
5. That's a clock.

F. Change to the singular.

EXAMPLE

Those are books.   *That's a book.*

1. Those are green buses.
2. These are oranges.
3. Those are apples.

4. These are brown desks.
5. Those are yellow tables.

G. Complete the sentences with the possessive adjective that refers to the subject of the first sentence.

EXAMPLE

Michael is a college student. ____*His*____ book is on the desk.

1. Sam Stern is a doctor. _____ pencil is on the desk.
2. I'm a teacher. _____ books are on the desk.
3. You're a student. _____ notebooks are on the floor.
4. We're students. _____ pencils are on the desks.
5. Michael and Susan are students. _____ books are on the table.
6. Marta is a typist. _____ notebook is on the table.
7. Mr. Lee is a lawyer. _____ book is on the desk.
8. You're nurses. _____ pencils are on the table.

H. Add *old* to these sentences and make any other changes that are necessary.

EXAMPLE

It's a notebook.   *It's an old notebook.*

1. They're tables.
2. They're pencils.
3. It's a car.

4. She's a cashier.
5. He's a driver.
6. It's a purse.

General Practice

Answer the questions.

EXAMPLE

Is that her book or her purse?
It's her purse. It's not her book.
Where is her purse?
It's on the floor.

1. Is that his book or his pen?
   Where is his book?

2. Is that your pen or your pencil? (my)
   Where is your pen?

3. Are those your pens or your pencils? (our)
   Where are your pencils?

4. Is this my book or my notebook? (your)
   Where is my notebook?

5. Is that her book or her notebook?
   Where is her notebook?

6. Are those their books or their notebooks?
   Where are their books?

7. Is that his notebook or his pen?
   Where is his pen?

8. Are those her pencils or her notebooks?
   Where are her notebooks?

LESSON

SIX

Reading and Oral Practice

A. Listen and repeat.

Is there a clock in the classroom?
Yes, there's a clock in the classroom.
It's on the wall.

Is there a map in the classroom?
Yes, there's a map in the classroom.
It's on the wall.

Is there a calendar in the classroom?
Yes, there's a calendar in the classroom.
It's on the wall.

Is there a book on my desk?
There are two books on your desk.

Is there a notebook on your desk?
There are three notebooks on my desk.

How many pens are there in his pocket?
There's one pen in his pocket.

How many doors are there in the classroom?
There are two doors in the classroom.

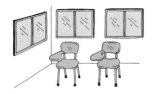

How many windows are there in the classroom?
There are three windows in the classroom.

How many students are there in the classroom?
There are four boys and five girls in the classroom.

How many pencils are there on the desk?
There are four pencils on the desk.

How many is used to ask questions about number.
Note that the plural form is used in the question
even when the number in the answer is *one*.

How many books are there on the table?
There's one book on the table.

B. Answer the questions.

How many calendars are there on the wall?
There's one calendar on the wall.

1. How many maps are there on the wall?

2. How many doors are there in the classroom?

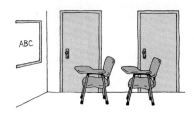

3. How many windows are there in the classroom?

4. How many pencils are there in his pocket?

5. How many books are there on the floor?

2+4=6   How much are two and four?
Two and four are six.

3+4=7   How much are three and four?
Three and four are seven.

4+4=8   How much are four and four?
Four and four are eight.

3+6=9   How much are three and six?
Three and six are nine.

4+6=10   How much are four and six?
Four and six are ten.

> *How much* is used in this lesson to ask questions about quantity, as in arithmetic questions.
>
> How much are one and two?
> One and two are three.

D. Answer the questions.

How much are one and one?
One and one are two.

$$1+1=2$$

1. How much are two and one?

$$2+1= \text{ ?}$$

2. How much are three and one?

$$3+1= \text{ ?}$$

3. How much are three and two?

$$3+2= \text{ ?}$$

4. How much are three and three?

$$3+3= \text{ ?}$$

5. How much are one and six?

$$1+6 = \text{ ?}$$

6. How much are three and four?

$$3+4= \text{ ?}$$

7. How much are three and five?

$$3+5 = \text{ ?}$$

8. How much are five and four?

$$5+4= \text{ ?}$$

9. How much are five and five?

$$5+5 = \text{ ?}$$

10. How much are four and six?

$$4+6 = \text{ ?}$$

Structure and Pattern Practice

> *There is* (*There's*) and *There are* are used to introduce expressions with an unidentified noun and a phrase giving location or place. In other words, instead of saying "A clock is on the wall," we say, "There's a clock on the wall." We use *There's* before a singular noun and *There are* before a plural.
>
> There's a calendar on the wall.
> There are two maps on the wall.

A. Complete with *There's* or *There are*.

EXAMPLE

___There's___ a chalkboard in the classroom.

1. _____ a notebook on the table.
2. _____ a clock on the wall.
3. _____ six boys in the classroom.
4. _____ nine girls in the classroom.
5. _____ a map on the wall.

B. Change to the plural. Add the number indicated in place of *a* or *an*.

EXAMPLE

There's a book on the table. (3)   *There are three books on the table.*

1. There's a girl in the classroom. (6)
2. There's a chair in the classroom. (10)
3. There's a desk in the classroom. (8)
4. There's a boy in the classroom. (9)
5. There's a purse on the table. (7)

C. Change to the singular. Substitute *a* or *an* for the number.

EXAMPLE

There are three notebooks on the table.   *There's a notebook on the table.*

1. There are ten tables in the classroom.
2. There are four oranges on the floor.
3. There are seven boys in the classroom.
4. There are nine girls in the classroom.
5. There are three old books on my desk.

> In questions, *is* and *are* come before *there*.
>
> Is there a calendar on the wall?
> Are there two or three maps on the wall?

D. Change to questions. Change *my* to *your*.

EXAMPLE

There's a chalkboard in the classroom.   *Is there a chalkboard in the classroom?*

1. There's a clock on my desk.
2. There are three books on the chair.
3. There's a calendar on my desk.
4. There are four apples on the table.
5. There are six notebooks on the floor.

Pronunciation and Intonation Practice

A. Repeat several times.

    a as in *that*: classroom, apple, an, am, map
    u as in *bus*: one, a, the, much
    e as in *ten*: desk, many, seven, pen, pencil, where, there
    i as in *it*: is, in, six, it's, Bill, his

B. Listen and repeat.

> **EXAMPLE**

There's a cal endar on the wall.

There are two oranges on the table.

1. There's a chalkboard in the classroom.
2. There's a clock on the wall.
3. There are four apples on the table.
4. There are two boys in the classroom.
5. There are three girls in the classroom.

General Practice

A. Answer the questions.

1. Are there five or six chairs in the classroom?

2. Are there six or seven girls in the classroom?

55

3. Are there four or five boys in the classroom?

4. Are there nine or ten books on the floor?

5. Are there two or three maps on the wall?

6. Are there three or four windows in the classroom?

7. Are there four or five pencils in his pocket?

8. Are there two or three pens on her desk?

9. Are there four or five apples on the table?

10. Are there nine or ten books on the chair?

B. Conversation. Give *real* answers to these questions or to others like them that your teacher will ask.

How many desks are there in this classroom?
How many students are there in the classroom?
How many windows are there?
How many doors are there?
Is there a chalkboard in the classroom?
Is there a map on the wall?
Is there a clock on the wall?
Is there a calendar on the wall?
How many books are there on your desk?
How many notebooks are there on your desk?
How many pens are there on your desk?
How many pencils are there on your desk?

Reading and Oral Practice

A. Listen and repeat.

Is there a desk in this office?
Yes, there is.

Is there a telephone on the desk?
Yes, there is.

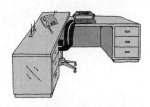

Is there a book on the desk?
No, there isn't a book on the desk.

How many drawers are there in the desk?
There are six drawers in the desk.

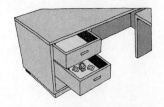

Are there any stamps in the top drawer?
No, there aren't any stamps in the top drawer.
There are some stamps in the middle drawer.

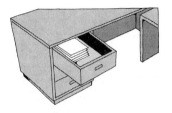

Is there any paper in the middle drawer?
No, there isn't any paper in the middle drawer.
There's some paper in the top drawer.

Are there any envelopes in the top drawer?
No, there aren't any envelopes in the top drawer.
There are some envelopes in the bottom drawer.

Is there a cup on the desk?
Yes, there is.

Is there some water in the cup?
No, there isn't any water in the cup.
There's some coffee in the cup.

Is there a purse on the floor?
No, there isn't a purse on the floor.
There's a purse on the chair.

B. Answer the questions.

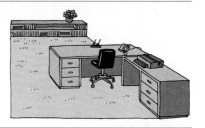

1. Is there a desk in this office?
2. Is there a telephone on the desk?
3. Is there a book on the desk?
4. How many drawers are there in the desk?

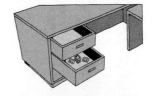

5. Are there any stamps in the top drawer?
   Where are there some stamps?

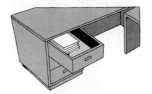

6. Is there any paper in the middle drawer?
   Where is there some paper?

7. Are there any envelopes in the top drawer?
   Where are there some envelopes?

8. Is there a cup on the desk?

9. Is there some water in the cup?
   What is there in the cup?

10. Is there a purse on the floor?
    Where is there a purse?

Is there a lot of milk in the glass?
No, there isn't much milk in the glass.
There's a lot of milk in the bottle.

Is there a lot of bread on the table?
No, there isn't much bread on the table.
There's a lot of bread in the kitchen.

Is there a lot of money on the desk?
No, there isn't much money on the desk.
There's a lot of money in her purse.

Are there a lot of keys on the desk?
No, there aren't many keys on the desk.
There are a lot of keys in his pocket.

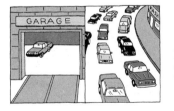

Are there a lot of cars in the garage?
No, there aren't many cars in the garage.
There are a lot of cars on the street.

Are there a lot of trucks on the street?
No, there aren't many trucks on the street.
There are a lot of trucks in the garage.

D. Answer the questions.

1. Is there a lot of milk in the glass?

2. Is there a lot of bread on the table?

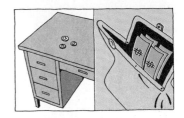

3. Is there a lot of money on the desk?

4. Are there a lot of keys on the desk?

5. Are there a lot of cars in the garage?

6. Are there a lot of trucks on the street?

Structure and Pattern Practice

> Negatives with *There is* and *There are* are formed by placing *not* after *is* or *are*. The contracted forms *isn't* and *aren't* are generally used in everyday conversation.
>
> > There is not (isn't) a telephone on the desk.
> > There are not (aren't) any books on the desk.
>
> *Some* is used after verbs in affirmative sentences. *Any* is used in negative sentences. Either can be used in questions.
>
> > There are some books on the table.
> > There aren't any notebooks on the table.

A. Change to the negative. Use the contracted forms. Change *some* to *any*.

EXAMPLE

There's some paper in the top drawer.   *There isn't any paper in the top drawer.*

1. There's some money in her purse.
2. There are some keys on the desk.
3. There are some cars in the garage.
4. There's some paper in the bottom drawer.
5. There are some envelopes in the bottom drawer.
6. There are some telephones in the office.
7. There are some desks in the classroom.
8. There's some coffee in the cup.
9. There's some bread in the kitchen.
10. There are some stamps in the top drawer.

There are two classes of nouns in English, count nouns and mass nouns. Count nouns are those that can be counted: *one book, two chairs, three tables*, and so on. Mass nouns refer only to things we do not usually count: *paper, milk, coffee, water, money*, and so on. Mass nouns are singular in form.

Much is used only with mass nouns. *Many* is used only with plural count nouns.

> There isn't *much milk* in the bottle.
> There aren't *many books* on the desk.

B. Complete these sentences with *isn't much* or *aren't many*.

EXAMPLE

There __isn't much__ water in the glass.

1. There _____ milk in the bottle.
2. There _____ stamps in the top drawer.
3. There _____ bread on the table.
4. There _____ coffee in the cup.
5. There _____ telephones in the office.
6. There _____ cars on the street.

Like *any, much* and *many* are generally used after verbs only in negative sentences. *A lot of* is the expression of number or quantity which is most frequently used in affirmative sentences.

> There are a lot of cars on the street.
> There aren't many trucks on the street.
>
> There's a lot of milk in the bottle.
> There isn't much milk in the glass.

Any of these expressions can be used in affirmative questions.

C. Change to the negative. Use contracted forms. Use *much* or *many*.

There are a lot of boys on the bus.   *There aren't many boys on the bus.*

1. There's a lot of milk in the glass.
2. There are a lot of trucks on the street.
3. There's a lot of bread in the kitchen.
4. There are a lot of stamps in the top drawer.
5. There are a lot of buses in the garage.
6. There's a lot of water in the glass.

D. Change to the affirmative. Change *much* or *many* to *a lot of*.

There aren't many boys on the bus.   *There are a lot of boys on the bus.*

1. There isn't much money in her purse.
2. There aren't many cars in the garage.
3. There aren't many stamps in the top drawer.
4. There isn't much coffee in the cup.
5. There isn't much paper in the bottom drawer.
6. There aren't many desks in the office.

Pronunciation and Intonation Practice

The contracted form *isn't* has two syllables, but the contracted form *aren't* has only one syllable.

A. Repeat several times.

is - n't   aren't

B. Repeat several times.

a as in *table*:   paper, they, eight
i as in *nine*:   five, I'm, my, white
e as in *ten*:   them, yes, desk, bread
o as in *no*:   notebook, those, window, also
u as in *you*:   blue, student, two, new

C. Listen and repeat.

EXAMPLE

There are some stamps in the drawer.

1. There are some books on the desk.
2. There's some water in the glass.
3. There's some paper in my desk.
4. There are some pencils in the drawer.
5. There's some milk in the bottle.

General Practice

A. Answer the questions with *not much* or *not many*.

EXAMPLE

Is there a lot of coffee in the cup?
No, there isn't much coffee in the cup.

1. Are there a lot of students in the classroom?

2. Is there a lot of money on the desk?

3. Are there a lot of stamps in the drawer?

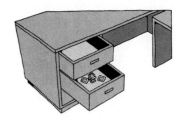

4. Are there a lot of oranges on the table?

5. Are there a lot of buses on the street?

6. Is there a lot of milk in the bottle?

7. Are there a lot of cars in the garage?

8. Is there a lot of water in the glass?

B. Answer the questions with *not any* and *some*.

Are there any keys on the table?
No, there aren't any keys on the table.
There are some keys on the desk.

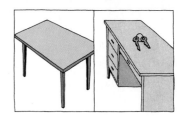

1. Is there any milk in the bottle?

2. Are there any trucks on the street?

3. Are there any books on the table?

4. Is there any bread on the table?

5. Are there any pencils in his pocket?

6. Are there any notebooks on the desk?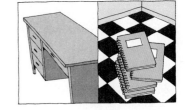

7. Is there any money on the desk?

8. Are there any envelopes in the top drawer?

C. Conversation. Give *real* answers to these questions or to others like them that your teacher will ask.

Are there any books on your desk?
Are there any notebooks on your desk?
Are there any pens on your desk?
Are there any pencils on your desk?
Are there any keys on your desk?
Are there any stamps on your desk?
Is there any money on your desk?
Is there any paper on the floor?
Is there any water on the floor?
Is there a clock on your desk?

Reading and Oral Practice

A. Listen and repeat.

Do you get up early every morning?
Yes, I get up at seven o'clock every morning.

Do you eat breakfast then?
Yes, but first I wash and dress.

Do you leave for school then?
I leave for school at eight o'clock.

Do you walk to school or take a bus?
I usually walk to school with my friend Pedro.

Do you and Pedro arrive at school at nine o'clock?
We usually arrive at school before nine o'clock.

B. Answer the questions.

1. Do you get up early every morning?

2. Do you eat breakfast then?

3. Do you leave for school then?

4. Do you walk to school or take a bus?

5. Do you and Pedro arrive at school at nine o'clock?

C. Listen and repeat.

Is Michael a high school or a college student?
He's a college student.

Does he get up early every morning?
Yes, he gets up at seven o'clock every morning.

What does Susan do?
She's a college student too.

What time does she get up?
She gets up at seven o'clock too.

Does Michael eat a big or small breakfast?
He eats a big breakfast.

Does Susan eat a big breakfast too?
No, she eats a small breakfast.

Does Michael leave for school at eight or nine o'clock?
He leaves for school at eight o'clock.

What time does Susan leave for school?
She leaves for school at eight o'clock too.

Does she take a bus?
No, she usually takes the subway.

What time does she arrive at the college?
She arrives at the college before nine o'clock.

What time does their first class begin?
It begins at nine o'clock.

What time is it now?
It's eleven o'clock.

1. Is Michael a high school or a college
   student?

2. Does he get up early every morning?

3. What does Susan do?

4. What time does she get up?

5. Does Michael eat a big or small breakfast?

6. Does Susan eat a big breakfast too?

7. Does Michael leave for school at eight or nine o'clock?

8. What time does Susan leave for school?

9. Does she take a bus?

10. What time does she arrive at the college?

11. What time does her first class begin?

12. What time is it now?

> *What time* is used to ask about time when the expected answer is in hours and minutes. Note that sentences that give time begin with *it*.
>
> It's eleven o'clock now.

E. Listen and repeat.

What time is it now?

It's twelve o'clock.
It's the middle of the day.
It's noon.

What time is it now?

It's twelve o'clock.
It's the middle of the night.
It's midnight.

What time is it now?

It's eight o'clock.

What time is it now?

It's ten o'clock.

PEDRO: Good morning, Mike.
MICHAEL: Good morning. How are you?
PEDRO: I'm fine, thank you. How are you?
MICHAEL: Fine, thanks.
PEDRO: Are we late?
MICHAEL: No, we're not. It's not nine o'clock yet.

Good morning is the usual greeting before twelve o'clock noon. *How are you?* is the customary question to ask about someone's health, and *I'm fine* is one of the customary answers. These greetings are usually very brief in English.

Mike is the nickname or shortened form of *Michael*.

Thank you is used to express gratitude. (*Thanks* is the short form.) *You're* (*you are*) *welcome* is the response.

Structure and Pattern Practice

The simple present tense of English verbs is formed from the basic (infinitive) form, as follows:

Singular	Plural
I leave	we leave
you leave	you leave
he leaves ⎫	
she leaves ⎬	they leave
it leaves ⎭	

Note that after *he, she,* or *it*—the third person singular—*s* or *es* is added to the verb.

walk, walks   leave, leaves   dress, dresses

The simple present tense is used for a customary or habitual action that takes place regularly in present time.

A. Complete the sentences with the correct form of the verb indicated.

EXAMPLE

Mike _____*gets*_____ (get) up at seven o'clock every morning.

1. You _____ (leave) for school at eight o'clock.
2. I _____ (get) up at seven o'clock every morning too.
3. Susan _____ (get) up at seven o'clock too.
4. We _____ (walk) to school every morning.
5. My friend _____ (take) the subway to college.
6. I _____ (wash) first and then I _____ (dress).
7. Mike _____ (eat) a big breakfast.
8. The bus _____ (arrive) before nine o'clock.
9. The boys _____ (leave) before nine o'clock.
10. School _____ (begin) at nine o'clock.

B. Substitute *he* for *I* in these sentences.

EXAMPLE

I get up at seven o'clock every morning.   *He gets up at seven o'clock every morning.*

1. I wash first.
2. Then I dress.
3. I walk to school.
4. I leave for school at eight o'clock.

C. Substitute *she* for *you* in these sentences.

EXAMPLE

You get up at six o'clock every morning.   *She gets up at six o'clock every morning.*

1. You take the bus to school.
2. You arrive at school before eight o'clock.
3. You begin school at eight o'clock.
4. You eat a small breakfast.

> Questions begin with the auxiliary verb *do*. The form *does* is used with *he, she,* or *it*.
>
> | *Singular* | *Plural* |
> |---|---|
> | Do I begin . . . ? | Do we begin . . . ? |
> | Do you begin . . . ? | Do you begin . . . ? |
> | Does he begin . . . ? | |
> | Does she begin . . . ? } | Do they begin . . ? |
> | Does it begin . . . ? | |

D. Change to questions.

EXAMPLE

I get up at seven o'clock every morning. (you)   *Do you get up at seven o'clock every morning?*

1. He eats a big breakfast.
2. She eats a small breakfast.

3. Mike walks to school with his friend Pedro.
4. They arrive at the college before nine o'clock.
5. The bus arrives at school before nine o'clock.
6. We take the subway to school. (you)
7. The buses leave for the college at eight o'clock.
8. Susan gets up before seven o'clock.
9. I eat a big breakfast. (you)
10. His first class begins at nine o'clock.

> Note that *it* is used as a subject to substitute for
> things that are neuter in fact, whereas *he* is used
> only for males and *she* only for females. There is,
> in other words, no grammatical gender in
> English. *They* is the plural form for all three.
>
> *School* begins at nine o'clock.
> *It* begins at nine o'clock.
>
> *The buses* arrive before nine o'clock.
> *They* arrive before nine o'clock.

E. Change the subject of these sentences to the appropriate personal
pronoun.

EXAMPLE

The bus leaves at eight o'clock.   *It leaves at eight o'clock.*

1. Susan gets up at seven o'clock.
2. The bus arrives at nine o'clock.
3. The students arrive at nine o'clock.
4. Michael eats breakfast at eight o'clock.
5. The class begins at ten o'clock.
6. The bus leaves at five o'clock.
7. The buses leave early in the morning.
8. Michael and Susan take a bus to school.

Pronunciation and Intonation Practice

A. Repeat several times. The *s* ending of verbs has three different pronunciations, like the plural form of nouns.

s	*z*	*iz*
walks	begins	washes
takes	leaves	dresses
eats	arrives	

B. Repeat several times.

th as in *the*:	then, they, there, that, this, these, those
th as in *thank*:	three
p as in *pen*:	pencil, pocket, cup, top, map
b as in *but*:	big, begin, before, bus, book
t as in *ten*:	to, top, table, take, it, that

C. Listen and repeat.

EXAMPLE

What time do you get up?

1. What time is it now?
2. What time do you eat breakfast?
3. What time do you leave for school?
4. What time do you arrive?
5. What time does school begin?

General Practice

A. Answer the question "What time is it?"

1.

6.

2.

7.

3.

8.

4.

9.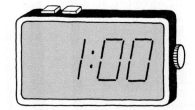

5.

10.

B. Answer the questions.

1. Is it noon or midnight?

2. Is it noon or midnight?

C. Conversation. Give *real* answers to these questions or to others like them that your teacher will ask.

1 What time do you get up?
2 Do you eat a big or a small breakfast?
3 What time do you leave for school?
4 How do you get to school?
5 What time do you arrive at school?
6 What time does school begin?
7 What's your first class?
8 What time does your English class begin?
9 How many students are there in your English class?

Reading and Oral Practice

A. Listen and repeat.

What's that young man's name?
His name is Richard Johnson. We call him Dick.

What does he do every day?
He works in an office in the city.

How does he go to work?
He goes to work by car.

Where does he live?
He lives on Cherry Street.

Does he live alone or with his family?
He lives with his family.

How many people are there in his family?
There are four people in his family.

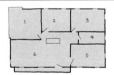

How many rooms does their house have?
It has six rooms.

What does Dick's father do?
He's a businessman. He works in the city.

What does Dick's mother do?
She's a nurse. She works in a hospital.

Does Dick have a brother?
No, he has a sister.

What's his sister's name?
Her name is Linda. She's a chemistry student.

Note the *-s* form of these verbs: to have–has; to do–does; to go–goes

I *have* a sister. He *has* a brother.
I *do* my work. He *does* his work.
I *go* to college. She *goes* to college too.

Fathers and *brothers* are always masculine in English, and *sisters* is always feminine. *People* is plural and is used with plural verbs.

B. Answer the questions.

1. What's that young man's name?

2. What's your name?

3. What does Dick Johnson do every day?

4. What do you do every day?

5. How does he go to work?

6. Where does he live?

7. Does he live alone or with his family?

8. How many people are there in his family?

9. How many rooms does their house have?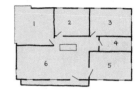

10. What does Dick's father do?

11. What does Dick's mother do?

12. Does Dick have a brother?

13. What's his sister's name?

8 + 3 = 11 How much are eight and three?
Eight and three are eleven.

8 + 4 = 12 How much are eight and four?
Eight and four are twelve.

9 + 4 = 13 How much are nine and four?
Nine and four are thirteen.

10 + 4 = 14 How much are ten and four?
Ten and four are fourteen.

8 + 7 = 15 How much are eight and seven?
Eight and seven are fifteen.

8 + 8 = 16 How much are eight and eight?
Eight and eight are sixteen.

8 + 9 = 17 How much are eight and nine?
Eight and nine are seventeen.

8 + 10 = 18 How much are eight and ten?
Eight and ten are eighteen.

8 + 11 = 19 How much are eight and eleven?
Eight and eleven are nineteen.

10 + 10 = 20 How much are ten and ten?
Ten and ten are twenty.

D. Answer the questions.

1. How much are nine and two? $9+2=?$

2. How much are nine and three? $9+3=?$

3. How much are six and seven? $6+7=?$

4. How much are seven and seven? $7+7=?$

5. How much are five and ten? $5+10=?$

6. How much are seven and nine? $7+9=?$

7. How much are seven and ten? $7+10=?$

8. How much are nine and nine? $9+9=?$

9. How much are nine and ten? $9+10=?$

10. How much are nine and eleven? $9+11=?$

PROFESSOR ELLIS:	Good afternoon, Pedro.
PEDRO:	Good afternoon, Professor Ellis. How are you today?
PROFESSOR ELLIS:	Very well, thanks. How are you?
PEDRO:	I'm fine, thank you.
PROFESSOR ELLIS:	Who's that young man?
PEDRO:	His name is Dick Johnson.
PROFESSOR ELLIS:	What does he do?
PEDRO:	He works in an office in the city.
PROFESSOR ELLIS:	Where does he live?
PEDRO:	He lives on Cherry Street.

Good afternoon is the customary formal greeting from twelve o'clock noon to about five o'clock in the afternoon. *Very well* is another customary answer to the question *How are you?*

Who is used to ask questions about people. *Who's* is a short form for *Who is.*

Who works in that office? *Dick* works there.

Structure and Pattern Practice

> The possessive form of singular nouns is formed by adding *'s* to the noun.
>
> boy – boy's   girl – girl's   Dick – Dick's

A. Complete each sentence with the correct possessive noun form.

EXAMPLE

_____*Mike's*_____ house is very small. (Mike)

1. _____ house is small too. (Dick)
2. _____ books are on the floor. (Pedro)
3. The _____ pen is on her desk. (teacher)
4. _____ house is very small. (Mrs. Johnson)

> Remember that the *-s* form is used in the present tense when the subject is a singular noun or *he, she,* or *it.*

B. Substitute *she* for *I* in these sentences.

EXAMPLE

I leave for school at eight o'clock.   *She leaves for school at eight o'clock.*

1. I work in the city.
2. I live on this street.
3. I have a big house.
4. I go to college.

C. Substitute *they* for *he* in these sentences.

EXAMPLE

He lives on this street.   *They live on this street.*

1. He leaves for school at eight o'clock.
2. He arrives at school before nine o'clock.
3. He takes the subway to work.
4. He has two sisters.

Remember that *do* or *does* comes before the subject in questions in the present tense. The simple form of the main verb is always used after *do* or *does*.

D. Change to questions.

EXAMPLE

He lives on this street.   *Does he live on this street?*

1. He lives alone.
2. They go to a big college.
3. I go to a college in the city. (you)
4. We have our first class at ten o'clock. (you)
5. The bus leaves before eight o'clock.
6. She has two brothers.

Questions that begin with question words have the same order as questions that ask for a *yes*-or-*no* answer—that is, the auxiliary *do* or *does* comes before the subject.

What time does your first class begin?
What time do they arrive at school?

What does he do? What does she do? asks for a person's occupation.

What does Mrs. Johnson do?   She's a nurse.

E. Change to questions beginning with the question words indicated.

EXAMPLE

The bus leaves at eight o'clock. (what time)   *What time does the bus leave?*

1. I work in an office. (where) (you)
2. He works in the city. (where)
3. I have two brothers. (how many) (you)
4. She lives on this street. (where)

5. His first class begins at nine o'clock. (what time)
6. We get up at six o'clock. (what time) (you)
7. This house has eight rooms. (how many)
8. I eat breakfast at seven o'clock. (what time) (you)

Pronunciation and Intonation Practice

A. Repeat several times.

oo as in *book*:　good
ch as in *much*:　chair, teacher, chalkboard
sh as in *wash*:　she, cashier
　d as in *do*:　does, doctor, day, door, desk
　h as in *he*:　have, has, house, his, her, how
　f as in *four*:　five, floor, fine, first, family, father

B. Listen and repeat.

EXAMPLE

That's Mike's book on the table.

1. Those are your notebooks on the floor.
2. That's Dick's book on the floor.
3. That's my book on the chair.
4. That's your pen on the desk.
5. That's Susan's pencil on the desk.

General Practice

Conversation. Give *real* answers to these questions or to others like them that your teacher will ask.

What's your name?
What do they call you?
What do you do?
Where do you live?
Do you live alone or with your family?
How many brothers do you have?
How many sisters do you have?
How do you get to school?
Where is your school?
What time does school begin?

TEN

REVIEW

Structure and Pattern Practice

A. Change to the plural. Add the number indicated in place of *a* or *an*.

EXAMPLE

There's a book on the floor. (5)   *There are five books on the floor.*

1. There's a girl in the classroom. (16)
2. There's a room in the house. (6)
3. There's a classroom in the school. (12)
4. There's a desk in the classroom. (20)

B. Change to the singular. Substitute *a* or *an* for the number.

EXAMPLE

There are five books on the floor.   *There's a book on the floor.*

1. There are two notebooks on the desk.
2. There are four old houses on this street.
3. There are three tables in the room.
4. There are seven oranges on the floor.

C. Change to questions. Change *my* to *your*.

EXAMPLE

There's a book on my desk.   *Is there a book on your desk?*

1. There are two maps on the wall.
2. There are eight rooms in my house.
3. There's a map on the wall.
4. There's a notebook on my desk.

D. Change to the negative.

There are some oranges in the kitchen.   *There aren't any oranges in the kitchen.*

1. There's some coffee in the cup.
2. There are some books on the floor.
3. There's some water in the glass.
4. There are some trucks in the garage.

E. Change to the negative. Use *much* or *many*.

There are a lot of apples in the kitchen.   *There aren't many apples in the kitchen.*

1. There are a lot of envelopes in the middle drawer.
2. There are a lot of girls on the bus.
3. There's a lot of milk in the bottle.
4. There's a lot of bread in the kitchen.

F. Substitute *she* for *you* in these sentences.

You get up at seven o'clock.   *She gets up at seven o'clock.*

1. First you wash.
2. Then you dress.
3. You leave for work at eight o'clock.
4. You take the subway to your office.

G. Substitute *we* for *he* in these sentences.

He gets up at seven o'clock.   *We get up at seven o'clock.*

1. He takes a bus to work.
2. He eats a big breakfast.
3. He works in an office in the city.
4. He arrives at the office at nine o'clock.

H. Change to questions.

He gets up at seven o'clock.   *Does he get up at seven o'clock?*

1. She lives on this street.
2. The bus arrives before nine o'clock.
3. They take a bus to work.
4. We get up early every morning. (you)
5. She lives in the city.
6. He leaves home at nine o'clock.
7. I take a bus to work. (you)
8. The boys eat a big breakfast.

I. Change to questions beginning with the question word indicated.

He gets up at seven o'clock. (what time)   *What time does he get up?*

1. I work in the city. (where) (you)
2. I have four brothers. (how many) (you)
3. We work in an office. (where) (you)
4. She has two sisters. (how many)
5. The buses leave at eight o'clock. (what time)
6. His father works in an office. (where)
7. They arrive at school at nine o'clock. (what time)
8. Their house has seven rooms. (how many)

J. Complete each sentence with the correct possessive form of the noun in parentheses.

_____*Mike's*_____ house is very big. (Mike)

1. His _____ pencils are on her desk. (sister)
2. _____ notebooks are in her room. (Ann)
3. _____ sister is in college. (Dick)
4. My _____ books are on the floor. (brother)
5. _____ house is on this street. (Mrs. Davis)

General Practice

A. Answer the question "What time is it?"

1.

2.

3.

4.

5.

6.

7.

8.

9.

10.

11.

12.

B. Answer the questions.

EXAMPLE

How much are five and three?   *Five and three are eight.*

1. How much are fifteen and five?
2. How much are six and nine?
3. How much are seven and eight?
4. How much are nine and eight?
5. How much are eleven and nine?
6. How much are four and five?
7. How much are six and ten?
8. How much are seven and nine?
9. How much are eleven and five?
10. How much are six and seven?

LESSON

11

ELEVEN

Reading and Oral Practice

A. Listen and repeat.

What time does Dick get home from work?
He gets home at ten o'clock at night.

Why does he get home so late?
Because he attends night school after work.

Why does he attend night school?
Because he doesn't like his job.

What is his job?
He's the mail clerk in his office.

What does he study at night school?
He studies computer programming.
He also studies accounting.

Does he like both his subjects?
He likes computer programming. He doesn't like accounting.

Does he live near his school?
No, he doesn't live near his school. He lives a long way from his school.

Does he take a bus home after school?
No, he doesn't take a bus home after school. He drives home.

Does he have a new car?
No, he doesn't have a new car. He has an old car.

The verb *to like* is used in English the same as any other verb. The subject is usually a person, and the object is the person, place, or thing which is liked.

Dick likes computer programming.
He doesn't like accounting.
Ann likes her teacher.

The object of *to like* can be an infinitive.

He likes to study.
He doesn't like to walk to work.

B. Answer the questions.

1. What time does Dick get home from work?

2. What time do you get home from school?

3. Why does Dick get home so late?

4. Why does he attend night school?

5. What is his job?

6. What does he study at night school?

7. Does he like both his subjects?

8. Does he live near his school?

9. Do you live near your school?

10. Does Dick take a bus home after school?

11. Do you take a bus home after school?

12. Does he have a new car?

C. Listen and repeat.

$$\begin{array}{r} 10 \\ +20 \\ \hline 30 \end{array}$$

How much are ten and twenty?
Ten and twenty are thirty.

How do you count from twenty-one to thirty?
Twenty-one, twenty-two, twenty-three, twenty-four, twenty-five, twenty-six, twenty-seven, twenty-eight, twenty-nine, thirty.

$$\begin{array}{r} 11 \\ +20 \\ \hline 31 \end{array}$$

How much are eleven and twenty?
Eleven and twenty are thirty-one.

$$\begin{array}{r} 10 \\ +30 \\ \hline 40 \end{array}$$

How much are ten and thirty?
Ten and thirty are forty.

$$\begin{array}{r} 10 \\ +40 \\ \hline 50 \end{array}$$

How much are ten and forty?
Ten and forty are fifty.

$$\begin{array}{r} 10 \\ +50 \\ \hline 60 \end{array}$$

How much are ten and fifty?
Ten and fifty are sixty.

$$\begin{array}{r} 10 \\ +60 \\ \hline 70 \end{array}$$

How much are ten and sixty?
Ten and sixty are seventy.

$$\begin{array}{r} 10 \\ +70 \\ \hline 80 \end{array}$$

How much are ten and seventy?
Ten and seventy are eighty.

$$\begin{array}{r} 10 \\ +80 \\ \hline 90 \end{array}$$

How much are ten and eighty?
Ten and eighty are ninety.

$$\begin{array}{r} 10 \\ +90 \\ \hline 100 \end{array}$$

How much are ten and ninety?
Ten and ninety are one hundred.

1. How do you count from twenty-one to thirty?

?

2. How much are eleven and twenty?

11+20=?

3. How much are ten and thirty?

10+30=?

4. How do you count from thirty-one to forty?

?

5. How much are ten and forty?

10+40=?

6. How much are ten and fifty?

10+50=?

7. How much are ten and sixty?

10+60=?

8. How much are ten and seventy?

10+70=?

9. How much are ten and eighty?

10+80=?

10. How do you count from ninety-one to one hundred?

?

Whose car is that? It's
Dick's car.

Whose purse is this?
It's that young woman's purse.

Whose office is this?
It's Dr. Stern's office.

Whose keys are those?
They're my sister's keys.

Whose books are these?
They're Susan's books.

Whose stamps are these?
They're Mrs. Nakama's stamps.

Whose is a question word that asks about possession.

Whose desk is this?   It's Dick's desk.

F. Answer the questions.

1. Whose purse is this?

2. Whose keys are those?

3. Whose office is this?

4. Whose books are these?

5. Whose stamps are these?

6. Whose car is that?

PEDRO:	Good evening, Professor Ellis.
PROFESSOR ELLIS:	Hello, Pedro. How are you this evening?
PEDRO:	I'm okay. How are you?
PROFESSOR ELLIS:	All right, thanks.
PEDRO:	What time does your class begin?
PROFESSOR ELLIS:	At seven o'clock.
PEDRO:	Then we're not late yet.
PROFESSOR ELLIS:	No, not yet. The bus usually arrives early.
PEDRO:	That's good. I don't like to hurry.
PROFESSOR ELLIS:	And I don't like to be late.

Good evening is the customary formal greeting from about five o'clock in the afternoon until bedtime. *Okay* and *all right* are additional customary answers to *How are you?* Both are more colloquial than *very well* or *fine.*

Hello is a familiar greeting that can be used at any time of the day or night.

Note the use of the infinitive *to be* after *like.* This is the first use of the basic form *be.*

Structure and Pattern Practice

> The negative of the present tense is formed with *don't* (*do not*) and *doesn't* (*does not*) plus the basic form of the verb.
>
> | | |
> |---|---|
> | I don't begin | we don't begin |
> | you don't begin | you don't begin |
> | he doesn't begin | |
> | she doesn't begin } | they don't begin |
> | it doesn't begin | |
>
> Please note carefully that the basic form of the verb—without *s*—is used after both *don't* and *doesn't*.
>
> The contracted forms are almost always used both in conversation and writing.
>
> Note the -*s* form of the verb *to study* and other verbs that end with a consonant and *y*.
>
> study, stud*ies*   hurry, hurr*ies*

A. Change to the negative.

EXAMPLE

He likes to study.   *He doesn't like to study.*

1. She likes accounting.
2. We attend school every day.
3. I live near the school.
4. They live in a big house.
5. He drives to the city every morning.
6. Night school begins at seven o'clock.
7. You have a brother.
8. They study computer programming.
9. She gets up at six o'clock every morning.
10. I hurry to work.

B. Substitute *he* for *I* in these sentences.

I don't like to study.   *He doesn't like to study.*

1. I don't attend class every day.
2. I don't eat a big breakfast.
3. I don't hurry to work.
4. I don't study accounting.
5. I don't have a sister.

C. Substitute *you* for *she* in these sentences.

She doesn't like computer programming.   *You don't like computer programming.*

1. She doesn't like apples.
2. She doesn't eat a big breakfast.
3. She doesn't have a big family.
4. She doesn't live on this street.
5. She doesn't like the class.

Remember that *whose* asks about possession.

D. Change to questions with *whose*.

That's Dick's desk.   *Whose desk is that?*

1. Those are my keys.
2. That's my sister's car.
3. This is Professor Ellis's computer.
4. These are Susan's stamps.
5. That's Mr. Lee's office.

Pronunciation and Intonation Practice

A. Repeat several times.

> *j* as in *job*:   Johnson, orange, Mrs. Jones
> *s* as in *this*:   Miss, Sam, clocks, maps, wants, seven
> *z* as in *is*:   his, she's, pens, goes, does
> *sh* as in *she*:   she's, wash
> *ch* as in *much*: chair, teacher, chalkboard

B. Listen and repeat.

EXAMPLE

Does he like to study?   No, he doesn't like to study.

1. Does she like accounting?   No, she doesn't like accounting.
2. Do you walk to school?   No, I don't walk to school.
3. Does he work in the city?   No, he doesn't work in the city.
4. Does she attend high school?   No, she doesn't attend high school.
5. Do they arrive early?   No, they don't arrive early.

General Practice

Conversation. Give *real* answers to these questions or to others like them that your teacher will ask.

Do you get up at _____ ?
Do you leave for school at _____ ?
Do you walk to school?
Does school begin at _____ ?
Do you have your English class at _____ ?
Do you study _____ ?
Do you walk home?
Do you have a car?
Whose book is that?
Whose notebook is that?
Whose purse is that?

TWELVE

Reading and Oral Practice

A. Listen and repeat.

Give him a pencil.
Don't give him a pen.
Why does he want a pencil?
He wants to copy the sentences.

Give her a pen.
Don't give her a pencil.
Why does she want a pen?
She wants to write a letter.

Give them the books.
Don't give them the notebooks.
Why do they want the books?
They want to read the lesson.

Give me the magazine.
Don't give me the book.
Why do you want the magazine?
I want to look at the pictures.

Please give me a notebook.
Why do you want a notebook?
I want to copy the new words.

Please give me a cup.
Why do you want a cup?
I want some coffee.

Please give me a glass.
Why do you want a glass?
I want some milk.

Please give us the package.
Why do you want the package?
We want to open it.

Please give us the letters.
Why do you want the letters?
We want to read them.

Please show me the pictures.
Why do you want the pictures?
I want to look at them.

The verb *to want* can be followed either by a noun or an infinitive.

I want a pencil.
I want to write a letter.

B. Complete the sentences and answer the questions.

1. (Give him) _____ .
   (Don't give) _____ .
   Why does he want a pencil?

2. (Give her) _____ .
   (Don't give) _____ .
   Why does she want a pen?

3. (Give them) _____ .
   (Don't give) _____ .
   Why do they want the books?

4. (Give me) _____ .
   (Don't give) _____ .
   Why do you want the magazine?

5. (Please) _____ .
   Why do you want a notebook?

6. (Please) _____ .
   Why do you want a cup?

7. (Please) _____ .
   Why do you want a glass?

8. (Please) _____ .
   Why do you want the package?

9. (Please) _____ .
   Why do you want the letters?

10. (Please) _____ .
    Why do you want the pictures?

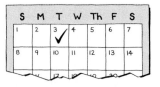

There are seven days in a week.
Monday is the first workday in the week.

Tuesday follows Monday.

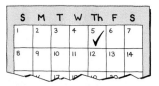

Wednesday comes after Tuesday.

Thursday is the day after Wednesday.

Friday is the last workday in the week.

Saturday and Sunday are the weekend.

People usually don't work on the weekend.
They usually stay home and rest.

D. Answer the questions.

1. How many days are there in a week?
2. What's the first workday in the week?

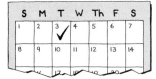

3. What day follows Monday?

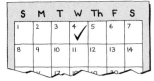

4. What day comes after Tuesday?

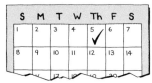

5. What's the day after Wednesday?

6. What's the last workday in the week?

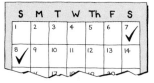

7. What days are the weekend?

8. Do people usually work on the weekend?

E. Dialogue.

DICK: Hello, Tom.
TOM: Hi, Dick. How are you?
DICK: I'm tired.
TOM: How come?
DICK: Too much work and too much school.
TOM: When do you go to school?
DICK: I go to school at night.
TOM: What do you study?
DICK: Computer programming.
TOM: Why do you want to study that?
DICK: I want to get a good job.
TOM: I want to get a good job too.
DICK: Come to my school!
TOM: Thanks. That's a good idea. Goodbye.
DICK: Bye.

Hi is a very informal greeting. It can be used at any time of the day or night.

How come? is used colloquially for *Why?* or *How did that happen?*

Too in this dialogue has the meaning of in *excess* rather than *also*, as it was used previously.

When is a question word that asks about time.

    When do you go to school? In the morning.

Goodbye is the customary leave-taking in English. It can be used at any time of the day or night. *Bye* is a short form, used informally.

Structure and Pattern Practice

IMPERATIVE. The imperative in English uses the basic form of the verb without any subject. The subject *you*, either singular or plural, is understood. Negative commands begin with *don't*, followed by the basic form of the verb.

Open the package now.
Don't open the package now.

A. Change these sentences to commands.

EXAMPLE

It's a good idea to walk to school.   *Walk to school.*

1. It's a good idea to drive to the city.
2. It's a good idea to eat a big breakfast.
3. It's a good idea to write the letters now.
4. It's a good idea to open the packages.
5. It's a good idea to take the subway.
6. It's a good idea to open the window.

B. Change these sentences to negative commands.

EXAMPLE

It's not a good idea to take the bus to work.   *Don't take the bus to work.*

1. It's not a good idea to read the letters.
2. It's not a good idea to copy the new words.
3. It's not a good idea to write the sentences.
4. It's not a good idea to read the lesson now.
5. It's not a good idea to study accounting.
6. It's not a good idea to open the door.

Polite commands, or requests, are usually introduced by *Please.*

Please give me a pencil.

C. Change these sentences to requests (polite commands).

EXAMPLE

I want you to drive the car to the city.   *Please drive the car to the city.*

1. I want you to hurry to class.
2. I want you to copy the new words.
3. I want you to write the sentences on the chalkboard.
4. I want you to open the package now.
5. I want you to give me the mail.

OBJECT PRONOUNS. The object pronouns in English follow verbs or prepositions (*to, at, on, in*, etc.).

Subject pronouns		Object pronouns	
I	we	me	us
you	you	you	you
he, she, it	they	him, her, it	them

D. Substitute the object pronoun for the *italicized* object in each sentence.

EXAMPLE

I take *the bus* to work.   *I take it to work.*

1. She drives *her father* to his office.
2. I walk to school with *Pedro.*
3. She writes *the new words* on the chalkboard.
4. Give *Susan* a pencil.
5. I want *the pen* now.
6. I walk to school with *Mike and Susan.*
7. I study *the lesson* every evening.
8. Give *the boys* their books.
9. He drives *his car* to work.
10. He drives *his mother* to work.

Pronunciation and Intonation Practice

A. Repeat several times.

u as in *bus*:	much, from, come, does, but, Monday, of
o as in *not*:	Tom, clock, job
a as in *all*:	office, walk, talk, wall, small
a as in *am*:	at, that, and, map, class, thank, have, has
a as in *day*:	late, ate, take, way, they
i as in *it*:	him, his, this, begin, big, city, give, live
i as in *time*:	Mike, arrive, fine, five, like, drive, night
e as in *ten*:	men, well, get, friend, then, yet, them, when
e as in *be*:	he, she, we, me, week, eat, street
o as in *no*:	so, those, old, go, alone, home, both

B. Listen and repeat.

EXAMPLE

Give him a pencil.   Don't give him a pen.

1. Count from twenty to thirty.   Don't count from one to twenty.
2. Open the package.   Don't open the letters.
3. Study computer programming.   Don't study accounting.
4. Copy the new words.   Don't copy the sentences.
5. Read Lesson Four.   Don't read Lesson Five.

General Practice

A. Answer the questions.

EXAMPLE

What day do they begin the new lesson?
They begin the new lesson on Monday.

1. What days does Dick work in the office?

2. What days of the week does Dick go to night school?

3. What days does Dick study computer programming?

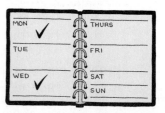

4. What days does Dick study accounting?

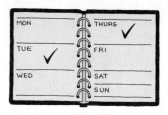

5. What days does Dick study English?

6. What days does Dick stay home and rest?

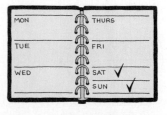

7. What day of the week does Susan have an early class?

8. What days of the week does Susan study
   English?

9. What day of the week do the college
   students have an early class?

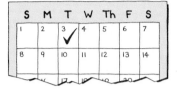

10. What days of the week don't the students
    have classes?

B. Conversation. Your teacher will ask you to perform actions like the one
   below and then ask you questions to which you should give *real* answers.

Please give _____ your book.
Does _____ have your book or your notebook?
How many books does _____ have now?
How many books do you have now?

LESSON

13

THIRTEEN

Reading and Oral Practice

A. Listen and repeat.

What did Mike do yesterday?
He attended his classes.

Is Mike a high school or a college student?
He's a college student.

What time did his first class start?
It started at a quarter after nine.

What time did the class end?
It ended at five after ten.

What time did his second class end?
It ended at noon.

What did Mike study yesterday morning?
He studied Spanish.

Did he attend classes in the afternoon too?
Yes, he attended English and history classes.

Why did Mike want to talk to his history professor?
He wanted to ask him about the homework.

Did the professor assign much homework?
Yes, he assigned a great deal of homework.

Did Mike finish all of the homework?
No, he didn't finish all of it. He finished only half of it.

Did Mike's professor excuse him?
No, he didn't excuse him. He assigned him extra homework.

1. What did Mike do yesterday?

2. Is Mike a high school or a college student?

3. What time did his first class start?

4. What time did the class end?

5. What time did his second class end?

6. What did Mike study yesterday morning?

7. Did he attend classes in the afternoon too?

8. Why did Mike want to talk to his history professor?

9. Did the professor assign much homework?

10. Did Mike finish all of the homework?

11. Did Mike's professor excuse him?

C. Listen and repeat.

It's five after two.

It's ten after two.

It's a quarter after two.

It's twenty after two.

It's twenty-five after two.

It's half past two.

It's twenty-five to three.

It's twenty to three.

It's a quarter to three.

 It's ten to three.

 It's five to three.

D. Answer the question "What time is it?"

1.

2.

3.

4.

5.

6.

7.

8.

9.

10.

11.

12.

PEDRO:	Why did you talk to the professor?
MIKE:	I wanted to ask him about the homework.
PEDRO:	What's the matter?
MIKE:	I didn't finish all of it.
PEDRO:	How much did you finish?
MIKE:	Half of it.
PEDRO:	Why didn't you do all of it?
MIKE:	I watched a movie on television.
PEDRO:	What did the professor say?
MIKE:	He assigned me extra homework.
PEDRO:	That's too bad.
MIKE:	Well, it's a good night to stay home and study.
PEDRO:	I know. I have a lot of mathematics and science homework.

What's the matter? is a question which is customarily used to ask about some kind of trouble or problem. *Well* is often used as an interjection at the beginning of a sentence, as in the next-to-last line of the dialogue.

Structure and Pattern Practice

The past tense of regular verbs is formed by adding *ed* or *d* to the basic form of the verb.

    talk, talk*ed*   arrive, arriv*ed*

Note the spelling of verbs that end in *y*.

    study, stud*ied*   hurry, hurr*ied*

The form for the past tense is the same for all persons.

I arrived	we arrived
you arrived	you arrived
he arrived	
she arrived	they arrived
it arrived	

A. Change these sentences to the past tense. Change the time expression to *yesterday.*

EXAMPLE

He attends his classes every day.   *He attended his classes yesterday.*

1. They copy the new sentences every day.
2. She watches television every night.
3. The buses arrive early every morning.
4. I talk to the professor every day.
5. He finishes the homework every day.
6. The class ends at noon every day.
7. The class starts at a quarter after nine every morning.
8. He assigns a great deal of homework every day.
9. The professor excuses him every day.
10. We study mathematics every day.

> Questions are formed with the auxiliary verb *did* (the past tense form of *do*).
>
> Did I start . . . ?   Did we start . . . ?
> Did you start . . . ?   Did you start . . . ?
> Did he start . . . ?
> Did she start . . . ? } Did they start . . . ?
> Did it start . . . ?

B. Change to questions.

EXAMPLE

The bus arrived early.   *Did the bus arrive early?*

1. The class started at nine o'clock.
2. I finished all of the homework. (you)
3. We stayed home on Sunday. (you)
4. I wanted to work in an office. (you)
5. She lived near the school.
6. The students counted from thirty to forty.
7. The boys walked to school yesterday.
8. The class ended at noon.
9. He studied computer programming at night school.
10. I liked my classes in college. (you)

C. Change to questions with the question words indicated.

EXAMPLE

The bus arrived before nine o'clock. (what time)   *What time did the bus arrive?*

1. We watched a movie on television. (what) (you)
2. We attended class on Saturday. (when) (you)
3. The class started at a quarter after nine. (what time)
4. I studied English in college. (where) (you)
5. She opened five packages yesterday. (how many)
6. The professor assigned a great deal of homework. (how much)
7. He wanted a pencil. (what)
8. He liked the book. (what)
9. He studied computer programming at night school. (where)
10. He stayed home on Tuesday. (when)

Negatives are formed with *didn't*, a contracted form for *did not*.

I didn't finish   we didn't finish
you didn't finish   you didn't finish
he didn't finish
she didn't finish }   they didn't finish
it didn't finish

The contracted form *didn't* is almost always used both in conversation and writing.

Note carefully that the basic form of the verb is always used after *did* and *didn't*.

D. Change to the negative.

EXAMPLE

The bus arrived late.   *The bus didn't arrive late.*

1. She thanked her teacher.
2. The students copied the new words.
3. The girls opened their books.
4. I stayed home on Sunday.
5. We attended a class Friday evening.
6. She asked the professor about the homework.
7. He assigned some homework.
8. They talked to the teacher.
9. I finished half of the homework.
10. The class ended before noon.

Pronunciation and Intonation Practice

A. Repeat several times. The -*d* ending for past tense regular verbs has three pronunciations—*d*, *t*, or a separate syllable.

d	*t*	*id*
stayed	walked	started
opened	talked	wanted
lived	asked	ended
arrived	watched	attended
assigned	finished	rested

B. Listen and repeat.

EXAMPLE

They copied the sentences.

1. I finished the homework.
2. They studied the lesson.
3. They studied the new words.
4. He assigned some homework.
5. She copied the sentences on the chalkboard.

C. Listen and repeat.

EXAMPLE

Why did they copy the sentences?

1. What did they watch on television?
2. Where did he attend school?
3. When did they live on this street?
4. What time did the class end?
5. Why did they watch television?

D. Listen and repeat.

Did they copy the sentences?

1. Did he assign a great deal of homework?
2. Did he attend school in the city?
3. Did they start the new lesson?
4. Did you stay home on Sunday?
5. Did you finish all of the homework?

General Practice

Conversation. Your teacher will ask you to perform actions like those below and then ask you questions to which you should give *real* answers.

Please walk to the door.
Did you walk to the window?
Please open the door.
Did you open the window?
Please open your book.
Did you open your notebook?
Please show _____ your pen.
Did you show him/her your pencil?
Please show _____ your notebook.
Did you show him/her your book?
Please show me your pencil.
Did you show me your pen?

LESSON
14
FOURTEEN

Reading and Oral Practice

A. Listen and repeat.

What did Dick do last night?
He went to school last night.

What kind of school does Dick go to?
He goes to a business school.

What time did his first class begin?
It began at six o'clock.

What classes did he have last night?
He had computer programming first.

Did he have accounting too?
No, he didn't have accounting.

What class did he have?
He had an English composition class.

What time did he get out of school?
He got out of school at half past eight.

Did he go home after school?
No, he didn't go home after school. He ate dinner at a restaurant near the school.

Did he go home after dinner?
No, he didn't go home after dinner. He went to the movies.

What kind of film did he see?
He saw a French film.

What time did he finally get home?
He finally got home at midnight.

B. Answer the questions.

1. What did Dick do last night?

2. What kind of school does Dick go to?

3. What time did his first class begin?

4. What classes did he have last night?

5. Did he have accounting too?

6. What class did he have?

7. What time did he get out of school?

8. Did he go home after school?

9. Did he go home after dinner?

10. What kind of film did he see?

11. What time did he finally get home?

C. Listen and repeat.

It's five after three.
It's three-oh-five.

It's ten after three.
It's three ten.

It's a quarter after three.
It's three fifteen.

It's twenty after three.
It's three twenty.

It's twenty-five after three.
It's three twenty-five.

It's half past three.
It's three thirty.

 It's twenty-five to four.
It's three thirty-five.

 It's twenty to four.
It's three forty.

 It's a quarter to four.
It's three forty-five.

 It's ten to four.
It's three fifty.

 It's five to four.
It's three fifty-five.

 It's four o'clock.

D. Give two answers to each question when possible.

1. What time did Susan get up?

2. What time did she eat breakfast?

3. What time did Susan arrive at school?

4. What time did her first class begin?

5. What time did her first class end?

6. What time did her second class begin?

7. What time did her second class end?

8. What time did she get out of school?

9. What time did she eat dinner?

10. She went to a movie. What time did the movie begin?

11. What time did she get out of the movie?

12. What time did she get home?

SUSAN: Did you see that new western movie?
DICK: Yes, I saw it last night.
SUSAN: Did you like it?
DICK: Yes, very much.
SUSAN: What time did you get out?
DICK: About midnight.
SUSAN: Did you walk home?
DICK: No, I had my car with me. I drove home.
SUSAN: You look tired today.
DICK: Well, yes I am, a little. But I had a good time.

What kind is an expression used to ask questions that expect an adjective as the answer.

What kind of film did you see?
I saw a French film.

But is used to connect contrasting ideas, often an affirmative and a negative.

Dick likes programming, but he doesn't like accounting.

To have a good time is a common idiomatic expression in English.

About in *about midnight* means approximately, near in time.

Structure and Pattern Practice

The past tense form of many verbs is irregular. These irregular forms do not follow any particular pattern, so it is necessary to memorize them. The past tense forms for the irregular verbs that have appeared in this book up to this point are:

begin, began	give, gave	read, read*
come, came	go, went	say, said
do, did	have, had	see, saw
drive, drove	know, knew	take, took
eat, ate	leave, left	write, wrote
get, got		

Otherwise, irregular verbs form the past tense the same way as regular verbs. Affirmative statements are the same for all persons.

I left	we left
you left	you left
he left	
she left }	they left
it left	

* The present *read* is pronounced like *reed*. The past *read* is pronounced like *red*.

A. Change these sentences to the past tense.

EXAMPLE

The class begins at ten fifteen.   *The class began at ten fifteen.*

1. The professor gives a great deal of homework.
2. He drives home from work.
3. I see movies on television.
4. I have a good time at school.
5. The English class comes after the science class.
6. The buses leave at eight-oh-five.
7. She takes the bus to work.
8. He gets up at seven o'clock.
9. We get out of work at four thirty.
10. He does a great deal of his work at home.

Questions are formed with the auxiliary verb *did*. The basic form of the main verb always follows *did*.

Did I begin . . . ?	Did we begin . . . ?
Did you begin . . . ?	Did you begin . . . ?
Did he begin . . . ?	
Did she begin . . . ? }	Did they begin . . . ?
Did it begin . . . ?	

B. Change to questions.

EXAMPLE

The class began at ten o'clock.   *Did the class begin at ten o'clock?*

1. They had their English class last night.
2. I saw the movie last night. (you)
3. He began school on Monday.
4. She got home at midnight.
5. He left the office at noon.
6. They ate at a big restaurant.
7. I gave him extra homework. (you)
8. We did the homework in class. (you)
9. The boys took a bus to the city.
10. She came to school by car.

C. Change to questions with the question words indicated.

EXAMPLE

I saw the notebooks on the teacher's desk.   *Where did you see the notebooks?*
(where) (you)

1. I saw my friend in the city. (where) (you)
2. He drove to the city on Saturday. (when)
3. He ate dinner at seven o'clock. (what time)
4. The professor gave a great deal of homework. (how much)
5. They read four lessons. (how many)
6. She came to work by subway. (how)
7. He got out of work at six o'clock. (what time)
8. He saw the movie on Tuesday night. (when)
9. We went home early on Thursday. (when) (you)
10. They had a house on this street. (where)

> Negatives are formed with *didn't*. The simple form of the main verb always follows *didn't*.
>
> I didn't come   we didn't come
> you didn't come   you didn't come
> he didn't come ⎫
> she didn't come ⎬   they didn't come
> it didn't come ⎭

D. Change to the negative.

EXAMPLE

The class began early.   *The class didn't begin early.*

1. I got home early last night.
2. He drove an old car to college.
3. She left the office at three o'clock.
4. I saw my friend on Wednesday.
5. I had a pencil in my pocket.
6. They took a bus to school.
7. She wrote her name on the chalkboard.
8. I wrote my friend a long letter.
9. They read the sentences on the chalkboard.
10. She ate a big breakfast this morning.

Pronunciation and Intonation Practice

A. Repeat several times.

d as in *did*:	old, stayed, friend, good, hundred, end, said
t as in *it*:	that, what, eight, get, eat, late, yet, about
r as in *or*:	her, our, your, were, there, for, door, car, father
l as in *all*:	small, wall, well, school, mail, hello, finally
b as in *be*:	big, job, bus, book, boy, begin, because, both
p as in *up*:	pen, apple, typist, pencil, map, pocket, copy
th as in *the*:	this, these, those, that, them, they, there
th as in *thank*:	three, thirteen, thirty, both

B. Listen and repeat.

Did they write the new words?   Yes, they wrote the new words.

1. Did she come to work by car?   Yes, she came to work by car.
2. Did he drive his new car?   Yes, he drove his new car.
3. Did they take English?   Yes, they took English.
4. Did you begin a new lesson?   Yes, we began a new lesson.
5. Did you see a movie?   Yes, I saw a movie.
6. Did she give him her book?   Yes, she gave him her book.
7. Did they leave at five?   Yes, they left at five.
8. Did you see her at school?   Yes, I saw her at school.

General Practice

A. Answer the questions.

1. What is the first workday of the week?

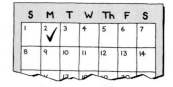

2. What day follows Monday?

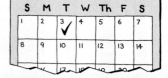

3. What day comes after Tuesday?

4. What day did Dick eat dinner at a restaurant?

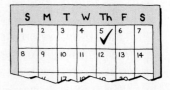

5. What's the last workday of the week?

6. What day did Dick stay home and rest?

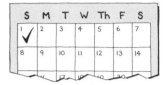

7. What day did Susan go to the movies?

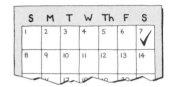

8. What days does Mike have his Spanish class?

9. What days does Mike study French?

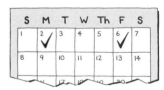

B. Conversation. Your teacher will ask you these questions or others like them. Give *real* answers to the questions.

Did you get up at _____ ?
Did you leave home at _____ ?
Did you drive to school?
Did you get to school at _____ ?
Did school begin at _____ ?
Did you have English at _____ ?
Did you leave school at _____ ?
Did you eat dinner at _____ ?
Did you go to school on _____ ?
Did you take English last year?
Did you see a movie last night?

REVIEW

Structure and Pattern Practice

A. Change to the negative.

EXAMPLE

She takes a bus to school.   *She doesn't take a bus to school.*

1. They study history.
2. He likes to get up early.
3. She works in an office.
4. I have a new car.
5. You talk to the teacher every day.
6. I finish all of my homework every day.
7. We eat a big breakfast.
8. She wants to watch television.

B. Change to the present tense.

EXAMPLE

She didn't want any coffee.   *She doesn't want any coffee.*

1. He didn't like accounting.
2. I didn't leave the office at five.
3. They didn't want to eat at a restaurant.
4. She didn't take the bus to work.
5. We didn't drive to school.
6. You didn't go to school on Saturday.
7. They didn't live in the city.
8. She didn't want to talk to the teacher.

C. Change these sentences to (1) commands, (2) negative commands, and (3) polite commands (requests).

EXAMPLE

He watched the mail clerk.   *Watch the mail clerk.*
Don't watch the mail clerk.
Please watch the mail clerk.

1. She gave the young man a job.
2. He carries the packages to the office.
3. She excused the students early.
4. I wrote the new words on the chalkboard.
5. We read the new lesson.

D. Substitute an object pronoun for the *italicized* object in each sentence.

EXAMPLE

He took *the bus* to work.   *He took it to work.*

1. She wants *the book* now.
2. I saw *Dick* at the restaurant.
3. I saw *Susan* at school.
4. He copied *the sentences* on the chalkboard.
5. He gave *his sister* a book.

E. Change to the past tense.

EXAMPLE

The bus arrives early.   *The bus arrived early.*

1. The professor excuses the students early.
2. We live in the city.
3. She works in an office.
4. I see a lot of movies on television.
5. He drives his car to work.
6. The class begins at ten fifteen.
7. He takes the subway to work.
8. The teacher writes the new words on the chalkboard.

F. Change to questions.

The bus arrived early.   *Did the bus arrive early?*

1. We rested on Sunday. (you)
2. I saw the letters. (you)
3. She went to the movies last night.
4. We hurried to the subway. (you)
5. They got up at eight o'clock on Sunday.
6. She left the office at four thirty.
7. I thanked the professor. (you)
8. We had a lot of mail yesterday. (you)

G. Change to questions with the question words indicated.

The bus arrived before nine o'clock.   *What time did the bus arrive?*
(what time)

1. We finished the lesson on Friday. (when) (you)
2. The teacher wrote the new words on the chalkboard. (what)
3. The teacher wrote the new words on the chalkboard. (where)
4. He carried the packages to the office. (where)
5. He got to school at seven forty-five. (what time)
6. They went to the movies on Saturday night. (when)
7. He gave us a lot of homework on Tuesday. (when) (you)
8. She came to work by bus. (how)

H. Change to the negative.

The bus arrived early.   *The bus didn't arrive early.*

1. They watched television last night.
2. I saw him at the office.
3. They took the subway to work.
4. He liked to drive in the city.
5. She saw him in the restaurant.
6. I gave my father the letters.
7. We read the words on the chalkboard.
8. We had a very good time.

I. Change to questions with *whose*.

They talked to Susan's professor.   *Whose professor did they talk to?*

1. I looked at Dick's books. (you)
2. She showed them Mike's picture.
3. He drove his sister's car to school yesterday.
4. They looked at Dr. Stern's office.
5. She attended Mrs. Jones's class last year.

General Practice

Conversation. Give *real* answers to these questions or to others like them that your teacher will ask.

What's your name?
What do you do?
Where do you live?
Where is your school?
What days do you have school?
What time do you usually get up?
What time did you get up today?
What time do you usually leave home?
What time did you leave home today?
How do you usually come to school?
How did you come to school today?
What time do you usually get to school?
What time did you get to school today?
What time does your English class begin?
How many students are there in the class?

Vocabulary

The following list includes the words introduced in Book 1. The number indicates the page on which the word first appears. If a word can be used as more than one part of speech, the way it is used in the book is as follows: n = noun, v = verb, adj = adjective, obj = object, pron = pronoun, poss = possessive, interj = interjection. If a word has more than one meaning or is part of a longer word or expression, the meaning or complete expression used in the book will be in parentheses.

a, 2
about, 123
accounting, 98
after, 98
afternoon, 90
all, 123
all right, 106
alone, 84
also, 11
am, 10
an, 38
and, 11
any, 58
apple, 38
are, 10
arrive, 70
ask, 123
assign, 123
at, 70
attend, 98

bad, 128
be, 106
because, 98
before, 70
begin, 73
big, 72
black, 16
blue, 15
book, 15
both, 99
bottle, 61
bottom, 59
boy, 49
bread, 61
breakfast, 70
brother, 85
brown, 15

bus, 15
business, 134
businessman, 85
but, 70
by, 84
bye (goodbye), 116

calendar, 48
call, 84
car, 38
cashier, 3
chair, 15
chalkboard, 24
chemistry, 85
city, 84
class, 73
classroom, 48
clerk, 98
clock, 38
coffee, 59
college, 6
color, 15
come, 114
composition, 135
computer, 98
cook (n), 3
copy, 110
count, 102
cup, 59

day, 76
desk, 24
dinner, 135
do, 70
doctor, 2
door, 24
Dr., 11, note
drawer, 58

dress, 70
drive, 99
driver, 3

early, 70
eat, 70
eight, 51
eighteen, 88
eighty, 102
eleven, 73
end (v), 122
English, 123
envelope, 59
evening, 106
every, 70
excuse (v), 123
extra, 123

family, 84
father, 85
fifteen, 88
fifty, 102
film (n), 135
finally, 135
fine, 77
finish (v), 123
first, 70
five, 49
floor, 34
follow, 114
for, 70
forty, 102
four, 49
fourteen, 88
French, 135
Friday, 114
friend, 70
from, 98